D0092643

OFF-KEY

poems by

Jean Esteve

Finishing Line Press
Georgetown, Kentucky

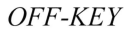

OFF-KEY

I S B N 1-59924-912-X / I S B N 978-1-59924-912-4 First Edition

ACKNOWLEDGMENTS

I would like to thank the following journals for their publication of individual poems in previous versions:

Florida Review: "Our Hero"
Faultline: "How You Stopped"
Harvard Review: "House of Ice"; "Off-Key"; "Sad Mountain"
Iowa Review: "A Capital Trip"; "Free of Hounds"; "I By the River";
        "The Night I Sang"
Lilliput Review: "Song"
Literal Latte: "April"
Literary Review: "Profile"
Madison Review: "Boys"
Plieades: "Found It"; "Idle Girl"; "STAT"
South Carolina Review: "Notebook: Her and Her Moths"
Walking Bridges Using Poetry as a Compass: "Walkway"
Zone 3: "Storm"

Editor: Leah Maines
Cover Art: Jean Esteve
Author Photo: Fred Harrison
Cover Design: Christen Kincaid

Printed in the USA on acid-free paper.
Order online: www.finishinglinepress.com
        also available on amazon.com

Author inquiries and mail orders:
Finishing Line Press
P. O. Box 1626
Georgetown, Kentucky 40324
U. S. A.

TABLE OF CONTENTS

3.   Song

4.   Idle Girl

5.   Off-Key

6.   Boys

8.   Found It

9.   I By the Riverside

10. STAT

11. Free of Hounds

12. Storm

13. Our Hero

14. Notebook: Her and Her Moths

15. Walkway

16. Ice

17. Profile

18. House of Ice

19. Poor Song

20. Daisies

21. Marigolds

22. The Pretty Garden

23. April

24. How You Stopped

25. The Night I Sang

26. A Capital Trip

27. Sad Mountain

To Mrs. Gooseberry, Mr. Kohl and Rabi,
wherever they may now be

Song

Didn't I sing to you, didn't I sing
leaves from their trees, and didn't I bring
sparrows down, too, until the country
lost summer, turned sullen. Didn't you hear me?

What did you think made your roadside so barren
except it be my relentless passion
for song. I was born with north wind in my voice.
I had no choice.

Dear boy, I had no choice.

Idle Girl

Sometimes I work
for a dollar or two
although few are the bosses
who like what I do.

Then I just sit
looking out, looking out,
at the boats in the bay
and the boys on the dock.

I can make herons
and good-luck charms
with nothing but beach grass
and colored yarn.

My parents are fretful
and tend to scold.
They think I should marry
but I don't know how.

Off Key

Sir, I was singing at myself
as a way to break the pace of work, A noon
song it was you overheard, not whispered words
to you. True, I was never good
at carrying a tune

and ideas fly by me like crows
in a murder
of anything laughable, anything giddy. Sir,
lurking in the shadows,
the noise you object to isn't a whimper

neither a psalm.
It's only a ditty aimed like the barrel
of a pistol at my own merry heart.

Boys

Dick Andrew is fugitive, Peter
loves me, and Jack is a rock.

      If tomorrow melts yellow
      with sunlight demanding
      that I be a sparrow

I'll brush by Dick lightly,
fly into the fluttering leaves

      where he'll never see me
      and there I will lay out
      my song

in patterns so tangled
he'll wonder his way
through the trees.

But in tempest and storm
it's a tortoise that I shall become

      shy and slow
      protected by occult beliefs
      and wit that is both dry and sweet.

Pete will be there
soaked in the rain
his coat pockets full
of live crickets to feed me

      though I'm restless, not hungry
      looking for Mike.

Why, Michael's been hiding
all this long time
beneath an umbrella

      his snickers expunged
      by a snarl of scrub oak

and I'll be a possum
while we exchange jokes

until I toddle on
to wait out the weather
on top of the rock.

Found It

Over here!
I've found it!
The path to happiness.

Bye-bye
blackbird,
bon nuit, trstesse.

Underneath the
brambles,
watch — don't tear your dress,

behind the
poison ivy
through the watercress,

lo! the Pond
of Riddles
whose shadows are dense

and whose vapors
are authentic
more or less.

I By the Riverside

I walked and walked
disturbing the river
that lurched alongside
the walkers' road.

"No one has walked
so fast so far
so far as I remember,"
the river roared.

Rivers do not
remember well.
Last year I walked
this far this fast myself.

A mind that's maimed
as much as mine, as you must know, has been,
needs months and months
of brisk walking.

I did not deign
to bicker, instead
I merely muttered,
Hush, river. Go to bed."

And, indeed,
it quieted.

Stat

The girl needs air.
Would someone please take her where
the trees are not so close together.

She's about to smother.
Surely there's another
region that can offer proper shelter.

Yonder is the most disarming ocean ever mapped.
It scampers back and forth like a sappy pet puppy,
soft to the touch, shiny, wet and threatless.

The girl is getting breathless.
She pulls buttons off her sweater
the way a chained pit bull strains out of its tether.

By the way, her name is Betty.
If you say it gently
she may not get so negative and jittery.

Would someone please invite her out to sea.
The water glitters.
How it differs from these rows and rows of trees.

Free of Hounds

Free of hounds leapt my spirit wooing
Dolores, Dolores my undoing.
Those spotted dogs took off after angry badgers.
I ran wild another way stalking a perfume.

She sprawled in the branches of a fall-colored tree
shook brilliant mash notes down on me.
Laughing, I devised an ivy ladder,
toes and ankles, thighs and so on dancing frivolously.

That the climb was hard alarmed me not at all, of course,
until she whispered me her name. Dolores.
I knew her mother. Now I know the daughter
and nothing good can be said for any of us.

Who adventures into happiness is by that much sadder.
The animals returned, full of badger, fatter.

Storm

I am away.
Call louder.
The wind is blowing
the wrong way.
It took our porch door
this morning.
It took down our fence.
It raked the clothes
right off the line
and now it wants mine,
the rags I'm wearing.
It wants me naked.

I've gone.
You'll have to yell
if you want my attention
and even then it's hard to tell
if I'll respond.
I'm looking for old toys
lost in the brambles,
lost under the sand.
A red plastic tractor,
a silver bear.
Where are they? Where are they?
I can't hear you.
They ought to be here.

If you find me,
I'll be naked
and you'll want me.
I want that tractor.
Come nearer. Come nearer,
The wind is winning
and the sand in collusion
carries blackberry branches
like standards.
Can you fix the fence?
Can you make a new door?
I don't know why
you insist on whispering.
I want that bear.

Our Hero

You had majesty enough
Astride once
Mink lap in satin breeches,
Glazed fold of fat across each thigh,
Hairs like eels, their silver mouths a-suck
at that I-know-who-I-am inside your skull.

When urgency returned we learned to loathe you.
We called you coarse, and worse,
We called you short.
We unhorsed you! cut your steed to ribbons!
Then carried you home beaming on our backs.

Notebook; Her and Her Moths

In sympathy with moths
that beat themselves silly against her window glass
she keeps the lights turned off
and nightly stumbles blindly through the house.

Walkway

Who does not stop
when crossing the bridge
over Alsea Bay
stop and look over
the delicate rail
to barnacled stones
old and patient
lying below.

Of those who stop
stop and gaze down
at long-weathered stones
who does not spit
then watch the lacy
delicate pellet
float toward the cold
gray water.

Of those who spit
over filigree breastwork
then let their gaze
follow its drift
who does not think
of themselves dressed in lace
winsome and delicate
hurtling downward.

Ice

Solstice. Ice
and crows.
Help me, I
can't reach him.
The phone lines
are frozen,
the roads
closed.
Blackbirds raise
a hellish noise.
Help. I won't
weather
such solstice
alone.

Profile

I said "That's not true,"
but my knees knew. They left me.
Down in the dust of the driveway I drew
with dumb hands and a blunt stick of wood
his profile as clear as I could.

A vain trick,
when we pretend our hearts are engines,
magical, fragile machines that feed us
pieces of rapture as long as we keep them engaged.
I learned the danger of fine-tuning mine.
Every fussy readjustment only
honed its own autocracy.

The lines in my driveway were shaky and limned
nobody I've ever seen.

House of Ice

Although warned by the wolf as well as the goose
not to make my home in a house of ice,
I've settled in here and I find it nice.
So there! So there! Dick Andrew.

Its windows are clear and stay tight shut
to allay my fear of thieves and such.
Indeed I like it here very much.
So there! So there! Dick Andrew.

The stove-fire burns deep ice-blue
and casts blue shadows across the floor.
I could not ask for any more
but you, but you, Dick Andrew.

Poor Song

If, then, we are to be poor,
let us do it in perfect squalor.
Let our kitchen swarm with cockroaches
and blackberries have at our yard,

Don't work happy
but pouring sweat
and desire for our iron bed.

If, then, we are to be poor,
let the nails spring loose from our front stoop,
where we can face each other naked,
swaying, bramble-scratched.

Daisies

Acres of daisies, a summer coverlet of white
with yellow polka-dots, not one worth the picking,
not one worth the bending over.
Daisies are anywhere. Who cares? They're sickening.
You know how sick those flowers are.

Billions of boys, a ballroom of Adam's apples,
ears that stick out fetchingly, ingenuous eyes blinking.
Not one worth bending over for.
Boys are born daily, smoking cigarettes and drinking beer.
You know how crude and mean boys are.

I would not even go downstairs to answer the doorbell
for a bouquet of florist's daisies sent me by a boy
if ever a boy thought of me that well.

Marigolds

He brought marigolds yesterday,
a rhinestone brooch the day before.
I sit in thought on my back porch
one day, two days older.

Vivacity of evening birds
fragments the brilliance of the setting sun
leaving splintered light, confetti on my lap.
I think in scraps
and love in even less remarkable cuttings.

Tomorrow he will bring a Hershey Bar
which I'll nibble, nodding Good,
good enough, my probable dear.

The Pretty Garden

He admired her garden as he passed,
      roses, begonias and daisies.
"Do you also like tea and cake?" she asked,
      roses, begonias and daisies.
She petted and pampered and purred at him,
and the very next week she married him.
A week after that she buried him,
      roses, begonias and daisies.

April

April air is milk, and
there's no getting away from the spill of it.
Nose, tongue, innards, even my legs
taste its thick liquid.

My neighbor hoots across the road to me.
"Pretty soon now.   Pretty soon and I'll bring you a boo-kay."
I salute him with gripped hands above my head,

salute the beady lilac buds whose shadows dot his bare pate.

On what day did the April boys
walk on by me toward my daughter?
When did their clear eyes cloud?

When the thrush settled elsewhere
leaving the pine trees deep in crows.

One day the mail box is stuffed with fliers
for tooth glue and pay-ahead graveyard plots.
I can bandy words with anyone
who lingers a while on the post-office steps.

All I ever get is ads. Fine weather. How's your mother.

What I want to do is clench his head between my fists and shout
look here a mouth is talking, kiss me,
or bring him home to show him what I own,
a tv, three new kittens, and a bureau drawer
full of silken underwear.

How You Stopped

...how you stopped by for breakfast, with poppies,
        and spread with shouts of scarlet beyond morning,
but when the tawdry flowers closed, didn't you, too —
        thin like sticks, the bunch of you
at night

The Night I Sang

What were you up to
the night I sang
with my pay in your pocket
and her on your pillow
giggling
among spermatozoa
and chocolate cookie crumbs?
What a mess of sheets
I had to launder
the weekend after
the night I sang
each verse of a song
whose tune I carried
all that night long.

A Capital Trip

We went for salmon,
me and him,
out past the last singing buoy,
on a choppy sea,
his wife aboard, too,
of course, as crew,
helpmeet, her feet
in high sturdy boots,
thick wool over all the rest.
I had on my flowery dress,
and like to froze
till he gave me his coat,
his big cozy jacket
right off his back,
when the wind whipped up
to a real squall
and rain fell hard
on the slippery deck,
rinsing my dainty hands.
We went for salmon,
came home with none,
no fish in the hold,
no wife in woolens,
a successful trip, nevertheless,
all told.

Sad Mountain

I took my time about
        climbing Sad Mountain.
No hurry. A road
        cut through alder and pine
then after a while just
        thatches of grass,
gold and wind-bent,
        but I took my time.

I stopped at a church
        on the side of Sad Mountain
drawn by loudness
        the cries of "Lord! Lord!"
A small congregation
        held armfuls of snakes,
most of them limp
        hung there complacent.

I left the service
        to listen for birds.
Not a chirp transpired
        and when I looked up
no flicker of wings
        but cloud and cloud only
gray all the way to the top.

I gave up my quest
        for the peak of Sad Mountain
or any other
        such far away going.
The down trip was harder
        steep and stony.
I bought me a soda when
        I achieved bottom.

Jean **Esteve** studied art at Cornell University School of Architecture. While there she wrote stories and features for the *Cornell Daily Sun* and the *Cornell Widow*. She became art editor of the *Cornell Widow*. Since then she has written for a variety of media, and in later years closed in on poetry in particular. Her poems have appeared in many American journals.